Original title:
The Magic Within

Copyright © 2024 Creative Arts Management OÜ
All rights reserved.

Author: Rory Fitzgerald
ISBN HARDBACK: 978-9916-90-112-0
ISBN PAPERBACK: 978-9916-90-113-7

Resonance of the Soul

In the silence deep and still,
Whispers echo, hearts fulfill.
Notes that dance upon the breeze,
Carrying dreams with gentle ease.

Each heartbeat sings, a sacred song,
Binding spirits where they belong.
In the shadows, light unfolds,
Unveiling truths that love beholds.

In the Realm of Possibilities

Where horizons stretch and bend,
Endless paths call out, ascend.
Stars align with fateful grace,
Every choice, a new embrace.

In the moments, time suspends,
Wonders wait around the bends.
Life's canvas waits for dreams to sow,
In this realm, let courage grow.

Flowing with Essence

Rivers carve their timeless way,
Reflecting sunlight, bright as day.
Nature's pulse, the heartbeats sway,
In this dance, we find our play.

Softly drifting, like the stream,
We merge as one, in flow, we dream.
With each current, we renew,
Essence of life, forever true.

An Enchanted Reverie

In twilight's hush, the magic stirs,
Echoing tales of distant blurs.
Dreamers wander in moonlit haze,
Lost in the spell of endless days.

Whispers linger, soft as sighs,
Painting visions in starlit skies.
Time suspends in realms of gold,
Each heart a story waiting to be told.

Secrets of the Spirited

In shadows deep, whispers arise,
Winds that speak of timeless skies.
A dance of light, where echoes play,
Secrets held in night and day.

Mysterious realms, where dreams align,
Silent guardians, spirits divine.
They weave a tale, both old and new,
Unraveling truths, for me and you.

Heart's Celestial Dance

In a cosmic waltz, the stars collide,
A rhythm found in the vast divide.
Every heartbeat sings a tune,
Lifted high by the silver moon.

As constellations twirl and sway,
Guiding souls along their way.
The universe hums a gentle song,
In this dance where we belong.

Quest of the Dreamweaver

With threads of hope, the weaver spins,
Crafting visions where life begins.
In realms of slumber, journeys start,
A tapestry born from the heart.

Through veils of night, the dreams unfold,
Stories whispered, secrets told.
The dreamweaver's touch, a gentle guide,
In endless worlds, we will abide.

Soul's Hidden Symphony

In quiet corners, melodies thrive,
Echoes of ancient voices alive.
Each note a journey, each chord a key,
Unlocking the essence of you and me.

The symphony swells in twilight's embrace,
A dance of souls in timeless space.
Harmony blooms in hearts that sigh,
As the music weaves us, you and I.

Echoes Through Time

Whispers of the past collide,
Memories like shadows glide.
Each moment holds a tale,
In twilight's gentle veil.

Footprints on the ancient ground,
In silence, truths are found.
The clock ticks on, yet still,
Time bends to its own will.

Voices call from ages old,
Their stories waiting to be told.
In the echoes, hearts align,
As we dance through space and time.

Tracing the Unseen

Beneath the surface, currents flow,
Mysterious paths we cannot know.
A touch, a glance, a fleeting sigh,
Invisible threads that tie and pry.

In shadows where the secrets linger,
Silent thoughts brush past our finger.
Casting nets in silent streams,
We seek the world that fuels our dreams.

Journeying through the quiet dark,
Finding paths with a gentle spark.
Trace the outlines of the soul,
In the unseen, we become whole.

The Hidden Kaleidoscope

Fragments of color dance and swirl,
Patterns shifting in a world unfurl.
Each twist reveals a story bright,
In the shimmer of morning light.

Hidden layers in each design,
A universe in pure align.
In chaos, beauty finds its way,
Through broken pieces, colors play.

Turn the lens, let visions blend,
A wondrous journey with no end.
Through the scope, we gaze anew,
Discovering worlds in every hue.

Embracing the Unknown

The horizon whispers soft and low,
Beyond the path we think we know.
With open hearts, we take a chance,
To leap into the wild dance.

Each step uncertain, yet so clear,
In the void, we shed our fear.
Brush against the fabric of fate,
In the unknown, we create.

Stars align in cosmic grace,
Guiding us to embrace space.
Hand in hand, through shadows roam,
In the unknown, we find our home.

Echoes of Hidden Dreams

In the silence, whispers creep,
Softly sighing, secrets keep.
Faded hopes in twilight's glow,
Echoes of what we do not know.

Beneath the stars, visions play,
Dancing shadows of yesterday.
Each breath holds a wish untold,
Dreams of silver, hearts of gold.

Voices linger, faint and light,
Guiding souls through darkest night.
Memory's touch, a gentle muse,
In hidden paths, we often choose.

Awake to find the morning's start,
A tapestry of the teeming heart.
In every beat, a story streams,
Life unfolds in hidden dreams.

Light Beneath the Surface

Underneath the calm of seas,
Lies a world of mysteries.
Rippling echoes, silken glow,
Light reveals what we don't know.

In shadows deep, the fish do hide,
Creatures dance with graceful pride.
Every wave a whispered tale,
Secrets linger in the pale.

Shimmering scales, a fleeting trace,
Nature's wonders, time and space.
In stillness, find a hidden spark,
Guiding us through depths so dark.

When the sun begins its rise,
Awakening the ocean's sighs,
We explore the realm so vast,
Finding treasures from the past.

Mysteries of Inner Realms

In the silence of the mind,
Endless pathways, all entwined.
Thoughts like rivers, flow and shift,
In the dark, the soul can lift.

Layers deep, the secrets hide,
Waves of feeling, ebbing tide.
Within the quiet, truths emerge,
Guided by an inner urge.

Visions dance in twilight's hue,
Peering through the veil of blue.
Every heartbeat's gentle call,
Whispers inspire us through it all.

Journey inward, seek the flame,
In the silence, know your name.
For the mysteries that you seek,
Are found in stillness, soft and meek.

Dance of the Unseen

In the shadows, movements glide,
Graceful forms that twist and slide.
With each beat, the world aligns,
In the dark, the spirit shines.

Voices echo in the night,
Calling forth the hidden light.
A ballet of the silent dream,
Flowing like a gentle stream.

Twirling stories, lost in time,
Rhythms rise, a silent chime.
Moments weave a sacred thread,
In the unseen, words unsaid.

Let the heart and soul embrace,
Moving through this sacred space.
In every whisper, every glance,
You will find the dance of chance.

Whispers of Enchantment

In twilight's soft embrace, we glide,
Where dreams and shadows gently bide.
A touch of magic in the air,
A symphony of souls laid bare.

With every heartbeat, secrets weave,
Within the hearts that dare believe.
Stars twinkle like the tales of old,
Their whispered promises unfold.

Beneath the moon's enchanting glow,
We dance where ancient rivers flow.
In every laugh and every sigh,
A world of wonder, you and I.

As night descends, the magic grows,
In every kiss, a story flows.
Entwined in dreams, we find our place,
In whispers shared, a sweet embrace.

Secrets in Starlight

Beneath the canopy of night,
Secrets shimmer, purest light.
Each star a story, softly told,
In whispers wrapped, a treasure gold.

The moonlight bathes the quiet ground,
Eternal echoes all around.
In silence, hearts begin to speak,
With every glance, the world unique.

Mysteries dance in cosmic flight,
Guiding souls through the endless night.
An inkling of fate in every glow,
In the starlit realm, our spirits flow.

Together lost in dreams divine,
We navigate the grand design.
In secrets shared, our bond we seal,
In starlit paths, our hearts reveal.

Heartstrings of Wonder

With every heartbeat, passions soar,
In tender moments, love's encore.
The tapestry of joy entwined,
In every glance, our souls aligned.

Through laughter shared and tears that fall,
We find our strength, we stand tall.
Each heartbeat echoes stories vast,
In heartstrings strummed, a spell is cast.

Whispers of hope in every song,
Together, where we all belong.
A melody of dreams takes flight,
In vast horizons, pure delight.

With open hearts, we journey on,
Through shadows cast, into the dawn.
In wonder found, we truly see,
The magic of our harmony.

Alchemy of the Soul

Transforming shadows into light,
With every breath, a pure delight.
The heart a vessel, deep and wide,
Where deepest truths and dreams collide.

In moments shared, our spirits blend,
The alchemy of love transcends.
With gentle hands, we mold the day,
Crafting joy in our own way.

In silence, wisdom starts to bloom,
Illuminating every room.
An inner fire that burns so bright,
Guiding us through the darkest night.

Together, weaving futures bold,
In alchemical tales retold.
In every heartbeat, we are whole,
The everlasting dance of soul.

Journey to the Extraordinary

A footstep forward, a dream ignites,
Paths uncharted, in starry nights.
With every turn, new wonders unfold,
In the heart of the brave, stories untold.

Mountains rise high, rivers flow deep,
In the whispering winds, secrets keep.
Guided by hope, we wander and roam,
In the journey, we all find a home.

Heartbeats of Illumination

In the silence, a pulse intertwined,
Each heartbeat echoes, souls aligned.
Flickers of light in darkness abound,
Through the shadows, new strengths are found.

Moments of truth, like stars in the sky,
In the chaos, we learn to fly.
With courage as fuel, we rise and ignite,
Guided by love, we embrace the night.

Serendipity's Embrace

Paths crossed gently, fate in a dance,
Unexpected moments, a whimsical chance.
Magic in laughter, joy in surprise,
In the tender embrace, our spirits arise.

A glance, a smile, the world feels right,
In the small things, we find pure light.
Guided by fortune through twists of time,
In the bend of the road, we find our rhyme.

Kaleidoscope of Possibilities

Colors swirl in a vibrant dream,
Life's a canvas, or so it would seem.
Each hue a story, each shade a voice,
In the dance of creation, we rejoice.

With every turn, new visions appear,
The beauty of change, something so dear.
In the spectrum of life, we paint our way,
Creating tomorrow from shades of today.

Colors of the Unimaginable

In a realm where shadows play,
Colors blend in disarray.
Dreams take flight on canvas bold,
Stories of the brave retold.

Each hue whispers tales untold,
Of distant lands and hearts of gold.
The spectrum sings a vibrant song,
In this world, where we belong.

A splash of red, a hint of blue,
A dance of green, a spark anew.
Palette rich, imagination flows,
In every stroke, the vision grows.

Whispers of Enchantment

Beneath the stars, a secret sigh,
The night is alive with soft lullaby.
Moonlight weaves through leaves so fine,
Whispers of magic in every line.

A breeze carries tales of the past,
Moments captured, forever to last.
Heartbeats echo in the still air,
Enchantment lingers everywhere.

Through the garden, shadows dance,
In every petal, a fleeting chance.
The world is painted, hues of delight,
Bathed in the glow of the shimmering night.

Secrets of the Heart

Within the chest, a treasure lies,
In silent dreams, the spirit flies.
Fragments of love, wrapped in time,
Echoes of laughter, sweet as a rhyme.

In tender glances, secrets bloom,
Hope and longing weave through the gloom.
Gentle whispers, soft as a sigh,
In the corners where true feelings lie.

The heart's soft map, a winding thread,
Guides us to the words unsaid.
In shadow and light, we search and seek,
In every pulse, the silent speak.

Veils of Wonder

In the mist of dawn, a soft veil falls,
Nature's whisper gently calls.
Mountains breathe in morning light,
Hidden beauty, pure delight.

Every petal holds a secret grace,
Veils of wonder softly embrace.
Time unwinds in fragrant air,
Magic dances everywhere.

Rivers glisten, reflecting dreams,
In their flow, life's beauty gleams.
Each moment wrapped in tender care,
Veils of wonder, beyond compare.

Glimmers in the Silence

In the hush of twilight's eve,
Whispers dance on gentle breeze,
Stars ignite, the world believes,
Hidden dreams find ways to tease.

Cloaked in shadows, secrets sigh,
Shimmering hopes float through the air,
Moments fleeting, they can fly,
Each heartbeat a silent prayer.

In the calm, a truth unfolds,
Echoes of what once was shared,
Glimmers bright, like threads of gold,
In our quiet, hearts are bared.

Listen close, the silence speaks,
In its arms, the world can heal,
Each soft note, a life that seeks,
Glimmers found in what we feel.

The Heart's Constellation

Stars align within our hearts,
Mapping love's celestial way,
Each pulse a dance, a work of art,
Guiding souls through night to day.

Nebulas of dreams ignite,
In the cosmos, hope is spun,
Shadows lost, replaced by light,
The heart's journey has begun.

Galaxies of laughter shine,
Orbits twist with every sigh,
In the quiet, love's design,
Paints our paths across the sky.

With each glance, a spark ignites,
Wonders bloom, horizons blaze,
In our gaze, the future writes,
The heart's constellation stays.

Wellspring of Untold Wonders

In the forest, dreams awaken,
Branches sway, a soft embrace,
Nature whispers, bonds unshaken,
Wonders bloom in every space.

Cascades of colors cascade down,
Each petal tells a story true,
Joy and hope can both be found,
In the morning's tender dew.

Depths of stillness, secrets gleam,
Rivers flow with ancient grace,
Every heart holds a hidden dream,
A wellspring of time and place.

Open eyes to every treasure,
In each moment, life unfolds,
Seek the beauty, find the measure,
Wellspring of wonders to behold.

Beyond the Boundaries of Perception

Waves of thought break on the shore,
Where the known meets the unknown,
Beyond the paths we walked before,
    The seeds of change are sown.

Veils of illusion drift away,
Truth unfurls like morning's light,
In silence, we begin to sway,
    To the rhythm of insight.

Chasing whispers, visions fly,
Into realms where limits cease,
In the heart, we find the why,
    Crafting wonders that release.

Beyond horizons, we inquire,
Into depths of endless grace,
In the vastness, we conspire,
    To explore time and space.

The Pulse of the Extraordinary

In shadows deep where dreams ignite,
Whispers dance in soft moonlight.
Each heartbeat carries tales untold,
In the stillness, magic unfolds.

The stars above, they shimmer bright,
Guiding souls through the velvet night.
A spark ignites, a vision clear,
In every silence, the pulse draws near.

Life's moments, both grand and small,
Echo with wonder, beckoning all.
With every breath, we chase the lane,
In the extraordinary, we find our flame.

So let us leap, let spirits soar,
For in our hearts, we crave for more.
The pulse of life beats wild and free,
A symphony of what's meant to be.

Hidden Wonders in Bloom

In quiet corners, secret blooms,
Whispers rise from ancient tombs.
Petals cradle morning's dew,
In their beauty, life feels new.

Beneath the soil where shadows play,
Hidden wonders find their way.
A gentle heart, a tender gaze,
Unfolds the magic of nature's maze.

With every bud that greets the sun,
Wonders awaken, one by one.
In silence, nature's story weaves,
A tapestry of what believes.

So take a moment, see the grace,
In every leaf, in every place.
For hidden wonders look to bloom,
In the embrace of life's sweet room.

The Spirit's Song

In the stillness, voices rise,
Carried softly through the skies.
A melody of hopes and dreams,
Flowing gently like silver streams.

Through valleys low and mountains high,
The spirit's song will never die.
Each note a whisper, pure and bright,
Dancing freely in the night.

In laughter shared and tears that fall,
The spirit's echo touches all.
A harmony of love that sings,
Connecting hearts with fragile wings.

So listen close, the heart will know,
The spirit's song can make us grow.
Through every joy and every pain,
Our souls unite, forever reign.

Threads of Ethereal Light

Gentle whispers in the dawn,
A tapestry of hopes reborn.
Woven dreams in colors bright,
Radiate with ethereal light.

Flickering soft in twilight's gaze,
Guiding souls through mystic ways.
Each thread spun from hearts so pure,
A bond unbroken, strong and sure.

In the silence, secrets gleam,
Painting visions in a dream.
With every shimmer, shadows play,
A dance of magic, night and day.

Embrace the glow, let it ignite,
In tender moments, clasp the light.
For in each thread, a story flows,
Of love and loss, of highs and lows.

Voices of Forgotten Spells

In ancient woods where whispers dwell,
Echoes weave a hidden spell.
Voices linger, soft yet strong,
Calling out, where hearts belong.

Beneath the moon's enchanting shine,
The magic of the night entwines.
Resonant chants of times long past,
In memories, enchantments cast.

Words once spoken, lost to years,
Emerge again through hopes and fears.
With every pulse, a chant resounds,
Awakening dreams in sacred grounds.

Listen close, the magic's near,
In every sigh, in every tear.
For forgotten spells are never lost,
They guide us through, whatever the cost.

Shadows that Sparkle

In the dusk, where the shadows play,
Sparkles dance and twirl away.
Glimmers soft, on edges thin,
Tales of wonder tucked within.

Beneath the stars, a secret glow,
Where light and dark collide and flow.
Mystic realms, where dreams ignite,
Each shadow holds a spark of light.

In the corners where fears reside,
Hope unfurls, a gentle guide.
For every dark, there's a bright spark,
Illuminating paths through the dark.

So venture forth, let spirits soar,
Find the sparkle, seek for more.
In every step, let shadows play,
For magic whispers, come what may.

Beneath the Veil of Ordinary

In daily life, where moments blend,
Lies a magic that will not end.
Beneath the veil, the mundane fades,
Revealing wonders, love cascades.

The rustle of leaves, a child's laugh,
In simple things, we find our path.
Eyes wide open, hearts untamed,
In quiet places, joy is claimed.

Every sunrise paints a new scene,
In the routine, the unseen gleans.
Moments fleeting, yet they stay,
In the tapestry of our day.

So cherish now, the little things,
For beneath the veil, true magic sings.
In every breath, there's beauty found,
In ordinary life, we are unbound.

Spark of the Enchanted

In twilight's glow, a whisper stirs,
A flicker kindles, twilight blurs.
Magic weaves through branches high,
In the heart where secrets lie.

Winds carry tales from days of old,
Of heroes brave and treasures gold.
Each dream ignites, a flame so bright,
Guiding souls through shadowed night.

Stars above, they wink and dance,
Inviting hearts to take a chance.
A spark ignites in every soul,
Embracing time, making us whole.

So let your spirit rise and soar,
Unlock the magic, crave for more.
With every breath, in reverie,
A spark enchanted, wild and free.

Dance of the Hidden

In the forest where shadows play,
Silent whispers lead the way.
Leaves entwine in a gentle sway,
Nature's song, a soft ballet.

Moonlit paths draw out the dreams,
In silver light, the magic gleams.
A dance begins, unseen to most,
Elusive spirits, we raise a toast.

Echoes of laughter swirl around,
Invisible feet upon the ground.
They twirl and spin, then fade away,
In the night, where secrets stay.

So listen close, the night speaks clear,
To those who wander, hearts sincere.
In stillness found, we move with grace,
A hidden dance in sacred space.

Radiance Beneath

Beneath the surface, life abounds,
In shadows deep, where peace surrounds.
Hidden gems of colors bright,
Waiting softly for the light.

Each heartbeat whispers ancient lore,
A tale of love worth waiting for.
In silence, strength begins to bloom,
A radiance dispelling gloom.

Roots intertwine in sacred ground,
Awakening the life profound.
Discoveries made with each new dawn,
Radiance found, our fears withdrawn.

So dive within, the treasures seek,
In quiet depths, the strong and meek.
What lies beneath, a spark of grace,
A radiance shines, a warm embrace.

Tapestry of Spirit

Threads of color, woven tight,
Stories echo in the night.
Each strand a tale, a moment spun,
A tapestry where all is one.

Patterns formed in love and strife,
A glimpse of each unique life.
Colors blend, both strong and weak,
In unity, our spirits speak.

With every knot, a bond is tied,
In joy and pain, we find our pride.
Together woven, hand in hand,
A quilt of dreams across the land.

So let the threads of hope unite,
In harmony, we take our flight.
The tapestry glows, a vibrant art,
A journey shared, one beating heart.

Heartstrings and Magic Dust

In twilight's glow, the stars align,
Whispers of dreams in the soft moonshine.
Threads of fate weave through the night,
Capturing hearts in their gentle flight.

With every brush of your tender grace,
Magic dust swirls in a silent space.
Binding us close, as the cosmos hums,
A symphony sweet, as our love becomes.

Beneath the sky, our spirits soar,
Wandering paths that hold so much more.
In laughter and tears, we share our way,
Heartstrings entwined, come what may.

So let the silence speak its truth,
In this dance of age and youth.
For every moment, we hold so dear,
Is painted bright by love's sweet veneer.

Beyond the Veil

In shadows deep, where secrets dwell,
A world unfolds, enchanted spell.
Veils of mist, soft whispers call,
Guiding the lost, embracing all.

Through moonlit paths, we wander free,
A journey woven with destiny.
Each step we take, the echoes play,
A song of souls that found their way.

Beyond the veil, in twilight's glow,
The heart knows paths we long to go.
In every breath, the magic flows,
A tapestry where true love grows.

So take my hand, let us explore,
The realms unseen, forevermore.
With every heartbeat, side by side,
Together we soar, our spirits guide.

Chords of the Ethereal

The essence of life, a gentle hum,
Chords of love, in harmony strum.
Through gentle breezes, our hearts entwine,
In this ethereal dance, so divine.

Melodies weave through the depths of night,
Notes take flight in the soft moonlight.
Each whisper shared, a sacred bond,
Resounds in echoes, of love's fond.

With every look, a thousand songs,
In symphonies sweet, where we belong.
A canvas painted in colors bright,
Chords of the soul glow in the night.

Together we sing, a vibrant tune,
Beneath the stars, beneath the moon.
In this embrace, let time stand still,
For love's perfect chords, our hearts fulfill.

A Dance with the Divine

In sacred spaces, where spirits meet,
We twirl and sway, gracefully fleet.
A dance with the divine beneath the stars,
Connecting souls from near and far.

The rhythm pulses, each heartbeat aligned,
Lost in the moment, hearts intertwined.
With every spin, the universe sings,
A celebration of all that love brings.

Illuminated by a soft, glowing light,
In this divine dance, all feels right.
Whirling through time, we cherish this chance,
An eternal waltz, a sacred romance.

So let us dance beneath the sky wide,
With faith in our steps, and love as our guide.
Together we'll flow, in a blissful trance,
Forever united, in this divine dance.

The Ripple of Possibility

A pebble dropped into a stream,
Sparks of dreams begin to gleam.
In quiet waters thoughts arise,
Infinite paths beneath the skies.

Each choice we make creates a wave,
Every heart has love to save.
In the stillness, echoes play,
Unseen journeys on display.

Fingers trace the shapes of fate,
Eyes are drawn to unseen gate.
With hope, we cast our fears aside,
In this moment, we confide.

What lies ahead, a mystery,
The ripple dances, wild and free.
A future bright, a whispered call,
Step by step, we rise or fall.

Journey into the Everdeep

Beneath the waves, the silence calls,
A world awaits in shadowed halls.
With each descent, the light does fade,
In depths unknown, fears masquerade.

The sirens sing their haunting tune,
Beneath the surface, hearts attune.
Through kelp forests, mysteries sway,
We seek the truth lost in the gray.

Echoes of the past resound,
In timeless currents, dreams abound.
With each stroke, the depths we claim,
As we explore the depths of shame.

A fragile dance with ghostly shades,
The sea embraces, never fades.
In every wave, a story speaks,
In darkened depths, our spirit seeks.

Emotions like Starlight

Soft whispers in the dark of night,
Emotions twinkle, pure and bright.
Like distant stars, they light the way,
Guiding hearts that want to stay.

A tender glance, a fleeting sigh,
In silence, love and pain do lie.
They sparkle like the falling rain,
In every joy, there lives the pain.

Moments captured, fleeting beams,
In every smile, a thousand dreams.
As galaxies of feeling swirl,
We dance beneath this cosmic pearl.

Yet shadows flirt with every light,
In joy, a hint of fragile fright.
In stardust glows the truth we find,
Emotions weave, forever bind.

Enigmas of the Heart

Hidden in the whispers deep,
Secrets of the heart do keep.
In gentle sighs and fleeting glances,
Love's great mystery advances.

Questions linger in the air,
What lies beneath the tender stare?
In silent moments, truths unfold,
The warmth of touch, a story told.

Layers of feeling intertwine,
In every heartbeat, clues align.
Yet, still, the search remains unclear,
For every joy, a shadowed fear.

Through twists and turns, we seek the key,
Unlocking hearts, we yearn to see.
In enigmas rich, we find our part,
The timeless dance of every heart.

A World of Subtle Wonders

In quiet glades where whispers play,
The dappled light begins to sway.
Each leaf a tale, each breeze a song,
In nature's arms, where we belong.

With twilight hues that softly blend,
The stars awake, their glow to send.
A tapestry of dreams unfolds,
In every heartbeat, life extols.

The river's mirror reflects the sky,
Where wishes drift and time slips by.
Mountains stand as silent guards,
In this realm of soft regards.

So let us roam these hidden trails,
Where wonder weaves its endless tales.
In subtlety, the heart shall find,
A world of treasures, intertwined.

Echoes of Enchantment

Through whispers soft, the night reveals,
A melody that gently seals.
In shadows cast by silver light,
The echoes dance, a sweet delight.

Beneath the moon's enchanting gaze,
Time slows down, the heart's ablaze.
Each shimmer sings of dreams untold,
As stories from the past unfold.

The forest breathes a timeless lore,
With every step, we seek for more.
In fragrant blooms and starlit skies,
Lies the magic that never dies.

So let us wander, hand in hand,
Through realms where dreams and truth expand.
In echoes deep, we shall embrace,
The enchantment of this sacred place.

Cradle of the Dreamer

In stillness, dreams begin to bloom,
A gentle hush, a whispered tune.
The cradle rocks, the stars align,
Where hopes take flight and hearts entwine.

With every sigh, the night unfolds,
A universe of tales retold.
In shadows cast by silver beams,
The cradle dances, sways in dreams.

The lullabies of twilight call,
In soft embrace, we rise and fall.
With every heartbeat, visions soar,
In dreamer's realm, forevermore.

So close your eyes, let visions steer,
In the cradle, shed your fear.
Together here, we find our way,
In realms where night and dreams hold sway.

Unfolding Fantasies

In gardens where the wildflowers sigh,
Fantasies weave, like clouds on high.
Each petal whispers of delight,
As colors dance in morning light.

Through secret paths where silence reigns,
Imagination breaks the chains.
A canvas bright with dreams to chase,
In every corner, magic's grace.

Beneath the arches of ancient trees,
The heart finds peace, the spirit frees.
With every breath, a story grows,
In unfolding dreams, the spirit flows.

So let us wander in this place,
Where fantasies meet time and space.
In every heartbeat, hope shall rise,
Unfolding wonders 'neath the skies.

The Symphony Within

In whispers soft, the notes resound,
A melody, both lost and found.
Harmony weaves through the soul,
Creating a rhythm, making us whole.

Each heartbeat plays a wild refrain,
Echoes of joy, of sorrow, of pain.
Together they merge, a vibrant song,
The symphony within, where we belong.

Notes of laughter dance in the night,
Strumming chords of pure delight.
In silence we hear the music clear,
An inner concert, drawing us near.

So close your eyes, let the music flow,
Feel every beat, let your spirit grow.
For in this realm, so rich and free,
Lives the symphony of you and me.

Tapestry of Marvels

Threads of wonder, woven tight,
Intricate patterns, colors bright.
Each story stitched, a tale to tell,
In the tapestry of marvels, we dwell.

Vibrant hues of joy and despair,
Textures of love, woven with care.
Moments captured in every seam,
Life's rich fabric, a living dream.

Patterns emerge, as life unfolds,
Wisdom in every stitch, so bold.
Together we stand, a brilliant array,
In the tapestry's warmth, we find our way.

So cherish each thread, and every fold,
For life's tapestry is a marvel untold.
Intertwined stories, forever alive,
In this wondrous weave, we all strive.

Radiance of the Unexplored

In shadows deep, where dreams reside,
There lies a spark we cannot hide.
The radiance waits, just out of view,
Calling the brave, the curious, the true.

Paths untraveled, whispers of fate,
Step into the light, it will not wait.
Daring hearts break through the mist,
To find the glow, they cannot resist.

Each glimmer a promise, each hue a chance,
To dance with the unknown, to take a stance.
Embrace the wild, set your spirit free,
In the unexplored, find the key.

So venture forth, let your courage soar,
For the radiance beckons, forevermore.
In every step, new wonders await,
In the realm of the unexplored, create your fate.

Journey to the Realm of Possibility

With open hearts and eager minds,
We seek a place where hope unwinds.
A journey awaits, both vast and wide,
To the realm where dreams can abide.

Each step a whisper, every choice a chance,
In this world of wonder, we dance.
Possibilities bloom like flowers in spring,
Coloring paths that courage can bring.

Mountains of doubt, we'll climb and face,
Trading our fears for a daring grace.
For here in the realm, where visions are spun,
We'll forge our futures, one by one.

So take the leap, let your spirit soar,
In the journey of life, there's always more.
To the realm of possibility, we will fly,
As limitless dreams embrace the sky.

Transcendence of Thought

Thoughts like stars in midnight's hush,
They sparkle bright, a gentle rush.
They weave a tapestry so deep,
Awakening dreams from silent sleep.

Floating high on wings of light,
Ideas dance, take graceful flight.
In every mind a world unfurls,
A cosmos spun from hidden pearls.

Whispers call from realms unknown,
A chorus formed from thoughts that've grown.
In the silence, truths take shape,
Endless paths our minds escape.

To transcend is to believe,
In what our hearts can weave and cleave.
A journey inward, vast and grand,
Where intellect and spirit stand.

Whirling in a Daze

Spinning round in circles tight,
Lost in echoes of the night.
Dreams collide in dizzying waves,
Fleeting moments, time enslaves.

Stars above begin to blur,
Thoughts cascade, a shiny spur.
The world dissolves in shades of gray,
As I twirl in sweet dismay.

Voices hum a hushed refrain,
A symphony of joy and pain.
In the whirlwind, I find grace,
In the chaos, my own space.

Every heartbeat, soft and loud,
Dazed yet clear amidst the crowd.
I'm a vessel, swirling free,
In this play, I just must be.

Whispers of the Unseen

Beneath the veil of silent nights,
Secrets murmur in the lights.
Breath of shadows, soft embrace,
Unseen beings leave a trace.

Echoes linger through the trees,
Carried softly on the breeze.
A world alive yet out of view,
Whispers brush against the blue.

Through the stillness, visions dance,
Enticing hearts with every chance.
Nature speaks in quiet tones,
Making magic from our bones.

What we see is just a part,
Of the wonders that we chart.
In the whispers, truth is found,
A symphony that knows no sound.

Portrait of the Imagination

Brushstrokes of a vivid mind,
Colors blend, a world defined.
Visions rise like morning sun,
Crafting tales that never run.

Through the canvas, dreams take flight,
Every shade a spark of light.
In the corners, shadows play,
Filling spaces day by day.

A lonely thought can shape a scene,
With quiet hopes that intervene.
Life emerges from abstract dreams,
A portrait crafted with moonbeams.

In each hue, a story spun,
Every glance a journey won.
Imagination, wild and free,
Paints a life for you and me.

The Spellbound Self

In whispered woods, where shadows play,
My thoughts unfold like leaves of May.
A gentle breeze, a secret told,
The heart's desire, a glimmering gold.

Through twilight's haze, I roam the night,
Chasing whispers, in soft moonlight.
Each step I take, a promise made,
In realms where dreams and wishes fade.

A tapestry of stars above,
Weaving tales of hope and love.
The spellbound self, lost in the glow,
A journey deep, where wildflowers grow.

In every breath, magic swells,
Awakening the hidden spells.
Eternal journeys, I'm bound to find,
In every moment, the magic binds.

Chasing Shadows of Delight

In the twilight's glow, shadows dance,
A fleeting moment, a whispered chance.
With laughter sweet, they slip away,
Chasing dreams at the end of day.

In gardens lush, where colors blend,
We seek the joys that never end.
Each step we take, a jubilant song,
Chasing shadows where we belong.

A fluttering heart, a playful sigh,
Underneath the sprawling sky.
We weave our fate, like threads of light,
In shadows' chase, our spirits ignite.

With whispers soft, we break the mold,
In every shadow, stories unfold.
Chasing delight through every night,
Our hearts, a canvas, painted bright.

Dreams that Dazzle

In the realm of dreams, I softly drift,
Where starlight glimmers, a precious gift.
With eyes closed tight, I see the beams,
Of wishes whispered within my dreams.

Floating clouds, like cotton candy,
In a world where everything's dandy.
With colors bright and laughter clear,
Each dream that dazzles draws me near.

Moments captured, like fireflies,
Twinkling softly, beneath the skies.
In a dance of joy, I find my way,
Lost in the magic, I choose to stay.

Through midnight's veil, my spirit roams,
In the land of dreams, I find my home.
Every heartbeat sings a song,
In dreams that dazzle, I truly belong.

A Symphony of Whimsy

In a world where laughter lives,
A symphony of whimsy gives.
With every note, a tale unfolds,
In colors bright and joys untold.

The dance of leaves in morning light,
Soft whispers echo, pure delight.
A melody crafted from pure play,
In whimsical rhythms, we find our way.

Like playful breezes, we twist and twine,
In carefree moments, hearts align.
With every giggle, the world ignites,
Creating magic on starry nights.

A symphony of hearts, we compose,
In laughter's embrace, our spirit glows.
With whimsy's touch, we'll always sing,
In harmony, all joy we bring.

Dreamcatcher's Whisper

In the night, a gentle sigh,
Woven stars, a lullaby.
Catch the dreams that drift and flow,
Hold them tight, let magic grow.

Feathers dance in moonlit air,
Binding dreams with tender care.
Whispers soft, they come alive,
In this heart, dreams learn to thrive.

Mystic visions intertwined,
A tapestry of hope defined.
Through the night, they weave their tales,
In their glow, the spirit sails.

With every dawn, the sunlight beams,
Awakens all our hidden dreams.
A dreamcatcher's sweet embrace,
Guides us to our destined place.

The Luminescent Inner Self

Glimmers rise from within the soul,
Bright reflections make us whole.
In the shadows, light will gleam,
Unraveling every hidden dream.

Colors burst, a vibrant hue,
Painting worlds both old and new.
Each heartbeat, a pulse of light,
Illuminates the darkest night.

Embrace the glow that sets us free,
In each strand of our history.
Spirit shining, ever bold,
A testament to stories told.

Dance in wonder, let it flow,
Champions of the inner glow.
For in the depths, we find our grace,
The luminescent, sacred space.

Sailing Through the Abyss

On the waves of darkened dreams,
Where silence swells and sunlight beams.
Set the sail and take the leap,
Into mysteries, vast and deep.

Stormy skies and calming seas,
Navigating with grace and ease.
Whispers echo in the night,
Guiding hearts towards the light.

Deepest waters, secrets dwell,
Each reflection holds a spell.
Past the horizon, treasures gleam,
Sailing forth on waves of dream.

With each breath, a new embrace,
Finding strength in time and space.
Through the abyss, our spirits soar,
In this journey, we explore.

Intentions in Bloom

In the garden, seeds we sow,
With intentions set to grow.
Petals whisper tales untold,
Of dreams and hopes, both brave and bold.

Sunlight kisses, rain descends,
Nature's touch, the heart transcends.
Each bloom tells a story deep,
In their fragrance, secrets keep.

Nurtured thoughts, like flowers rise,
Reaching out towards the skies.
In this dance, we find our way,
Intentions guide us day by day.

As seasons change, the colors fly,
A tapestry beneath the sky.
Watch them flourish, hearts attune,
Together, we are always in bloom.

Unraveling Mysteries

In shadows deep, secrets creep,
Whispers of time, a secret to keep.
Paths entwine with fate's design,
Searching the dark for the light to shine.

Questions linger in the night,
Chasing echoes, lost from sight.
Every riddle, a puzzle piece,
Yearning for answers that never cease.

As dawn breaks, the truth unfolds,
Stories hidden in tales retold.
Each moment, a step deeper still,
Unraveling the threads of will.

In the labyrinth, we find our way,
Guided by stars that lead to day.
With each heartbeat, we draw near,
To the answers we hold dear.

Glimpses of the Extraordinary

Beyond the veil of the mundane,
Lies a world both wild and untamed.
In fleeting moments, we find grace,
In the ordinary, a sacred space.

Colors burst in the morning dew,
Whispers of life, forever true.
Each smile shared, a spark ignites,
Turning shadows into lights.

From the mundane stems the divine,
In everyday life, treasures shine.
A child's laughter, a gentle breeze,
In these glimpses, hearts find ease.

So open your eyes to the unseen,
In the simple, find the serene.
Extraordinary waits for us all,
In every moment, heed the call.

Essence of Radiance

In stillness found, a glow appears,
A light that dances through our fears.
With every breath, a flicker grows,
Radiating warmth wherever it goes.

The heartbeat of the universe sings,
Melodies carried on gentle wings.
In the soul's embrace, we are one,
Basking in light from the sun.

Moments captured, forever bright,
Reflecting love in the softest light.
Each glance, a spark of divine grace,
Illuminating the human race.

Find the radiant within your core,
Let it guide you forevermore.
In each heartbeat, in every sigh,
The essence of radiance will never die.

Threads of the Soul

Weaving stories, threads intertwine,
In the fabric of life, a grand design.
Every encounter, a stitch of fate,
Binding us close, as we navigate.

From heart to heart, connections flow,
In silent whispers, we come to know.
Each thread a story, rich with lore,
In the tapestry, we find more.

Strength in unity, love in strife,
Threads of the soul, the fabric of life.
In joyous moments and in despair,
We rise together, stronger, aware.

So cherish each thread, each bond we make,
In this journey, the roads we take.
For in the weave, we find our whole,
The vibrant threads of the soul.

Flickers of the Sublime

In twilight's glow, the stars emerge,
Their whispers soft, a gentle urge.
The moon, a silver sentinel bright,
Guides lost souls through the endless night.

Veils of mist weave through the trees,
Carrying secrets on the breeze.
Each flicker sparks a thought divine,
Moments caught in the cosmic line.

Beneath the surface, stillness dwells,
A harmony that softly swells.
In silence, echoes of love reside,
In ripples vast, time's gentle tide.

We chase the light, we dance, we dream,
In realms beyond what we can seem.
The sublime whispers secrets true,
A tapestry of me and you.

Riddles of the Heart

The heart conceals its ocean deep,
In shadows where lost secrets seep.
Within the beats, a song unknown,
Yearning for warmth, but chilled to bone.

Gentle hands tracing lines of fate,
Each pulse a question, each breath a weight.
In tangled threads, our fates entwine,
A riddle whispered through the vine.

With every glance, a truth unfolds,
In silence, more than words have told.
We weave the moments, thread by thread,
In laughter born before we're dead.

Stars above reflect our tears,
In dreams, we conquer all our fears.
The heart speaks loud, the mind stands still,
In riddles of love, forever will.

The Shimmering Core

Deep in the earth, where shadows play,
Lies a core that lights the day.
With molten fire, it whispers low,
A dance of life in undertow.

The shimmering pulse of ages past,
A memory held, a shadow cast.
In the stillness, a vibrant roar,
Each tremor tells of ancient lore.

Through cracks and fissures, light breaks free,
A radiant blend of you and me.
The core ignites the darkest night,
In every heart, a hidden light.

From deep below, new worlds arise,
In fiery hues beneath the skies.
We are the echoes, we are the flame,
In the shimmering core, we find our name.

Pathways of Perception

In tangled forests, paths unfold,
With stories waiting to be told.
Each step reveals a new sunrise,
In hidden ways, the spirit flies.

Through twisting lanes, we search for truth,
In the innocence of youthful youth.
With open eyes, the world we trace,
In every moment, there's a grace.

Colors bleed, as shadows play,
In kaleidoscopes of night and day.
Perception shifts, a fleeting glance,
In the vastness, we find our chance.

The paths diverge, yet all unite,
In harmony, we chase the light.
Through endless journeys, we roam free,
In pathways bright, we learn to see.

Inward Odyssey

In shadows deep, I seek to find,
The whispers of my restless mind.
Through corridors of hope and fear,
I navigate, with dreams held dear.

Each step I take within my soul,
Unraveling the hidden whole.
The journey bends, the road unseen,
A tapestry of what has been.

The echoes of my past resound,
In this vast silence, truths are found.
A compass forged from joy and pain,
Guiding me through the mental rain.

Inward I travel, layers peel,
Discovering what's truly real.
In the depths, my spirit glows,
An odyssey that ever grows.

The Essence of Wonder

In twilight's glow, the stars awake,
A canvas vast, where dreams can take.
The whispers of the night unfold,
In mysteries both young and old.

With every breath, a new abyss,
A universe contained in bliss.
The flicker of hope, a fleeting spark,
Awakens hearts, ignites the dark.

Children gaze with wide-eyed grace,
In simple things, they find their place.
The essence lingers in their laugh,
In moments small, the greatest craft.

Let wonder bloom in every soul,
A timeless gift that makes us whole.
With open hearts and minds as free,
We dance within this mystery.

Guardians of the Soul

In quiet halls, where shadows tread,
The guardians watch, where spirits led.
They shield the light, they mend the cracks,
As we journey forth and trace our tracks.

With gentle hands, they guide our way,
Through stormy nights and brightened day.
Each whisper bold, a soothing balm,
Restoring peace, restoring calm.

Through life's tempest, they stand near,
The echo of a love sincere.
From ancient times, their wisdom flows,
In every heart, their strength bestows.

In gratitude, we hold them tight,
The shining sparks within the night.
Guardians true of every soul,
In unity, they make us whole.

Colors of the Invisible

In the hush of dawn, colors blend,
Shades of whisper, where dreams ascend.
Invisible strokes on canvas vast,
Paint the moments, futures cast.

A sigh of wind, a lover's glance,
In unseen hues, we find our dance.
The laughter shared, a silent song,
In colors bright, we all belong.

Through violet skies and emerald leaves,
We sense the touch, the heart believes.
Every heartbeat, a vibrant thread,
In the fabric of life, gently spread.

Look beyond what eyes perceive,
In the unseen, we learn to weave.
The colors bloom, the spirit grows,
In the invisible, love freely flows.

Alchemy of Dreams

In whispers soft, the night does weave,
A tapestry where dreams believe.
Each vision glows, a fleeting spark,
Transforming shadows, bright and dark.

Potions brewed from hopes and fears,
Glimmers caught in silvered spheres.
Awakening the soul's deep tune,
A symphony beneath the moon.

Wandering where the wild thoughts roam,
Crafting worlds that feel like home.
In hidden realms where secrets lie,
The heart takes flight, and fear runs dry.

In the alchemist's embrace, we find,
The magic of the dreaming mind.
With every breath, we shape the night,
In this celestial dance of light.

Echoes of Light

A gentle glow, a tender spark,
Resonates within the dark.
Whispers lull the weary heart,
As day and night begin to part.

Flickers tease the edges near,
Painting shadows, bright and clear.
Every echo, a story told,
In hues of warmth, soft and bold.

Waves of color dance and play,
Guiding lost souls on their way.
Through the silence, songs take flight,
Carrying dreams on wings of light.

In the stillness, we behold,
The magic woven, thread of gold.
Embracing all that shines so bright,
In the comforting echoes of light.

Threads of the Mystical

Weaving dreams on loom of fate,
Threads of magic intertwine, innate.
A tapestry of silken hue,
Each thread holds stories, old and new.

Dancing patterns shift and sway,
In the breath of night and day.
Mystical whispers in the air,
Lead wandering hearts with gentle care.

Colors merge in vibrant streams,
Carried forth on gossamer dreams.
Each stitch a journey, soft and shy,
Tracing paths where spirits fly.

In this fabric, truth is spun,
A tapestry where all are one.
Through threads of life, we come to see,
The magical weave of destiny.

Inner Realms Unveiled

In quiet depths, where shadows breathe,
A world unfurls, a tale to weave.
Layers peel, revealing light,
In inner realms of endless night.

Voices echo, softly call,
Inviting souls to rise and fall.
Through crystal caverns, thoughts will soar,
Unlocking keys to ancient lore.

Glimmers of truth dance all around,
In every heartbeat, wisdom found.
A journey mapped in stars above,
Illuminating paths of love.

As barriers fade, we start to see,
The wonders of our mystery.
In inner realms, we dare to roam,
And find within, our truest home.

The Unfolding of Dreams

In shadows deep where visions gleam,
A tapestry of hope we weave.
Each whisper stirs, ignites the flame,
Awakening the heart's sweet claim.

Gentle winds carry desires high,
Beneath the vast and watchful sky.
Each star a wish, a path to trace,
In silence, find our rightful place.

With every dawn, new colors flare,
The canvas shifts, potentials rare.
From slumber's grasp, we rise once more,
To chase the dreams we long explore.

In the night's embrace, we boldly leap,
Into the depths where secrets sleep.
For every dream that dares to rise,
A universe beyond the skies.

Spheres of Whimsy

Round the corner, laughter spins,
In fields of joy where life begins.
A dance of colors, bright and bold,
Stories shared, forever told.

In bubbles floating through the air,
Childhood whispers everywhere.
Each giggle springs like morning dew,
In circles drawn by me and you.

Collecting stars in jars of light,
Dreams painted in the soft twilight.
A realm where fantasy takes flight,
In spheres of whimsy, pure delight.

Paint your heart with every hue,
In this world, we start anew.
Let's chase the moments, unconfined,
Within this realm, our souls aligned.

The Inner Universe

Within the quiet spaces dwell,
A tapestry of tales to tell.
Stars flicker in the mind's expanse,
Inviting us to dream and dance.

In pathways forged of thought and time,
We navigate in rhythm and rhyme.
Each heartbeat echoes, softly sings,
The wonders that our spirit brings.

With every breath, a cosmos grows,
In shadows cast, an inner glow.
A journey through the silent night,
Exploring realms of pure insight.

In stillness, find the truth concealed,
The layers of the world revealed.
Our thoughts, like stars, in dark unfold,
The inner universe, bright and bold.

Touch of the Unfelt

A whisper carried on the breeze,
Connects our souls in gentle ease.
In moments shared, so soft, so frail,
The touch unseen, a silent trail.

Through fingertips, we find the way,
In shadows cast by light of day.
No need for words, just quiet grace,
In every heartbeat, find your space.

Eyes meet in silent understanding,
A realm of warmth and hearts expanding.
Each breath a bond, a sacred dance,
In this pure moment, take a chance.

The unspoken speaks in myriad tones,
A tapestry of love that moans.
In every glance, the world stands still,
With touches felt beyond mere will.

Reverie and Reality

In a dream I wander far,
With the moonlight as my guide.
Reality fades like a star,
As illusions gently glide.

Whispers of the night unfold,
Painting skies with pastel hue.
Stories waiting to be told,
In the silence of the blue.

Moments blend, reality bends,
Caught between the dawn and dusk.
Where the surface lightly ends,
And dreams wear a velvet husk.

But with dawn, the light will break,
Shattering the tranquil view.
Yet the dreams and memories make,
A tapestry forever true.

The Marvel Within

In the heart, a secret glows,
A flame that flickers, never dies.
Within the clouds, the essence flows,
Each thought a bright and wild surprise.

A gentle hand, it stirs the soul,
With every breath, a world reclaims.
In life's canvas, we are whole,
For in our hearts, the magic flames.

Unseen wonders, soft and sweet,
In the silence, we can find.
In every heartbeat, every beat,
The universe within our mind.

The marvel waits in all we do,
As petals open to the sun.
Embrace the whispers, know it true,
The greatest journey has begun.

Essence of the Elusive

Like shadows danced on twilight's veil,
Fleeting moments come and go.
Catching whispers in the gale,
The essence of the softest glow.

In the mist, a figure sways,
A ghost among the ancient trees.
In the dawn, the sunlight plays,
Sketching dreams upon the breeze.

A sigh escapes, an echo sings,
From the depths of uncharted streams.
In the silence, a soft wind brings,
The whispers hidden in our dreams.

Yet time obeys a fickle hand,
As footprints fade upon the shore.
The elusive calls, a distant land,
A journey worth pursuing more.

Captured in a Gossamer Web

In the morning dew, it glimmers bright,
Threads spun of silver, soft and fine.
A delicate dance, in pure sunlight,
Where moments linger, endlessly entwined.

Whispers caught in fragile strands,
Stories woven by the light.
With gentle care, it understands,
To cradle dreams both day and night.

Within the web, the world stands still,
A sanctuary for fleeting time.
Each glint a memory, each thread a thrill,
Nature's artistry, rhythmic rhyme.

Yet as the breeze begins to blow,
The web dissolves in morning's breath.
Yet in our hearts, its magic flows,
Capturing life, defying death.

Unraveling the Essence of Being

In whispers soft, the truth unfolds,
A journey mapped in fleeting gold.
Each breath a thread, each thought a seam,
We weave the fabric of our dream.

In shadows deep, reflections call,
The heart's soft echo, a gentle thrall.
With every note, we learn to sing,
The essence held in everything.

In mirrors clear, the self revealed,
In silence vast, our souls unsealed.
Through tangled paths, we seek the light,
In being whole, we find our sight.

The essence glows, a flame divine,
In fleeting moments, we intertwine.
In every touch, in every glance,
We unravel life, a sacred dance.

Flickers of the Extraordinary

In mundane hours, we find the spark,
A flicker bright, igniting the dark.
Each moment holds potential vast,
In simple sights, the spell is cast.

A raindrop's kiss on thirsty land,
The brush of grass, a gentle hand.
In laughter shared, in whispers low,
Extraordinary seeds we sow.

A glance that lingers, a shared sigh,
From shadows deep, our spirits fly.
Through everyday, the magic glows,
In tiny joys, true wonder grows.

These fleeting sparks, they guide our way,
Through hidden paths where dreamers play.
In every heart, a light resides,
Flickers of life, where magic abides.

Chasing Celestial Echoes

Beyond the stars, our dreams take flight,
In cosmic dance, we chase the light.
Each shimmer speaks of tales untold,
A universe of wonders bold.

In every pulse, the rhythm sways,
In starry dust, we find our ways.
With open hearts, we seek the sound,
Of echoes lost, in space unbound.

Through endless night, our spirits soar,
In galaxy's arms, we yearn for more.
With every wish cast to the skies,
We weave our fate, where fortune lies.

In astral realms, we chase our dreams,
In twilight's glow, the heartbeat schemes.
To touch the stars, is all we seek,
Chasing echoes, bold and unique.

Unseen Realities

Within the veil, where shadows blend,
Unseen worlds twist and extend.
In whispered thoughts, the unseen gleams,
A dance of truths, a weave of dreams.

We walk the line, a fragile grace,
In hidden realms, we find our place.
Through veils of mist, we glimpse the true,
In silent depths, the heart's anew.

In every breath, a mystery lies,
Beyond the veil, where spirit flies.
Through layers soft, our minds explore,
The unseen truths forevermore.

In quiet moments, revelations bloom,
In tender light, they chase the gloom.
With open eyes, we seek to see,
The unseen threads of reality.

Milton Keynes UK
Ingram Content Group UK Ltd.
UKHW021953151124
451186UK00007B/226